MAKEOVERS
AT THE
BEAUTY
COUNTER
OF
HAPPINESS

MAKEOVERS
AT THE
BEAUTY
COUNTER
OF
HAPPINESS

ILENE BECKERMAN

ALGONQUIN BOOKS OF CHAPEL HILL

2005

Published by
ALGONQUIN BOOKS OF CHAPEL HILL
Post Office Box 2225
Chapel Hill, North Carolina 27515–2225

a division of
WORKMAN PUBLISHING
708 Broadway
New York, New York 10003

Published simultaneously in Canada by Thomas Allen & Son Limited.
Design by Robbin Gourley.

Library of Congress Cataloging-in-Publication Data
Beckerman, Ilene, 1935–
     Makeovers at the beauty counter of happiness / by Ilene Beckerman.
     p. cm.
   ISBN-13: 978-1-56512-374-8
   ISBN-10: 1-56512-374-3
   1. Women—Psychology. 2. Self-esteem in women. 3. Beauty,
Personal—Psychological aspects. 4. Body image in women.
5. Feminine beauty (Aesthetics) I. Title.
HQ1206.B335 2005
306.4'613—dc22

                                                           2004062392

10 9 8 7 6 5 4 3 2 1
First Edition

Author's note: I changed the names of some of my characters.
Unfortunately, I couldn't change my own name.

Makeovers
at the
Beauty
Counter
of
Happiness

1958. The movie is *Vertigo*.
Kim Novak asks Jimmy Stewart, "Couldn't you
like me just the way I am?"

2001. The movie is *Bridget Jones's Diary*.
Renée Zellweger asks Hugh Grant, "Can't you just
like me the way that I am?"

A lot of things have changed since 1958.
Some things never change.

I have six granddaughters. They're all beautiful.
They don't think so. One doesn't like her nose, one
thinks her stomach isn't flat enough, one thinks her
hair is too flat. The list goes on.

The only one who doesn't complain about her looks
is the baby. She hasn't learned to yet. She's two.

I can identify with my granddaughters. I started
a list of things that were wrong with me a long
time ago. And I kept adding to it.

During my life, I've spent thousands of hours and
thousands of dollars on my hair, my makeup, and
my clothes, trying to look prettier because I grew up
believing that pretty girls had happier lives.

I'd be a lot happier now if I had that time and
that money back.

Dear Mother Teresa,

I have always been a fan of yours. If only I had used the time I've spent pursuing the beauty secrets of movie stars, supermodels, Jacqueline Kennedy, and Audrey Hepburn more wisely, I might have become more like you or Sandra Day O'Connor.

I just wish one of you had had Audrey Hepburn's wardrobe.

Your fan,
Ilene

I didn't send the letter.
I write a lot of letters I don't send.

I wrote this letter to my granddaughter Olivia on her eleventh birthday. I didn't send it either.

Dear Olivia,

When I was your age, I worried a lot about the way I looked. It wasn't until I got a lot older that I realized that Barbra Streisand's nose didn't get in the way of her becoming a superstar.

I hope you don't have to wait as long as I did to know nobody's perfect.

A million hugs and xxxxxxx's,
Grandma

P.S. If you don't know who Barbra Streisand is, ask your mother.

Soon after Olivia's eleventh birthday, I received a letter in the mail that made me remember myself at her age.

It was an invitation to my elementary-school class reunion.

You're Invited
Hunter Elementary School Class of 1947
REUNION
Remember the joys and sorrows of being eleven?
Please come to a memory mixer and special event.
We've contacted most of our classmates from
Lexington Avenue to Pacific Palisades
and have had an enthusiastic response.

It went on to give the date, time, and place—at the home of a girl who had never invited me to her birthday parties.

All the feelings of insecurity I had when I was Olivia's age came back to me when I read the invitation. I may not remember where I put my glasses five minutes ago, but I remember vividly how painfully shy I once was.

Dear Sofia Coppola,

You remind me of my dentist's daughter.
I was very happy when you won an Academy Award
for Lost in Translation but why did you wear
plain black flats to the Oscars? Do you have
foot problems?

You were the only person there who looked like
they didn't want to be there. Don't worry about your
shyness problem. I used to be shy, too.

Your fan,
Ilene

I had some pictures of my classmates in an old cordovan valise I had bought at a garage sale years ago. I was going to fix the handle some day. I dug out the valise and found the pictures.

I'm the tall one in the middle of the back row. Patty, on my right, was the pretty one. Ann, second row right, was the smart one. I could name everyone in the picture. I didn't think any of them would remember me.

Not many of my classmates signed my sixth grade autograph book . . . I was too shy to ask everyone. Most of the inscriptions in my book say "Good luck."

Everybody else's book said, "To my best friend," or had sayings like

> *Tulips in the garden,*
> *tulips in the park,*
> *but the tulips I like best*
> *are two lips in the dark.*

My class in 1947.

Dear Ann Landers,

I just got an invitation to my elementary-school reunion.

Last time I saw my classmates, I was eleven years old and had freckles. Now I'm sixty-five and have liver spots.

My problem is I still hate Tommy Berman because he made fun of me. If I go to the reunion, do I have to talk to him?

Your friend,
Confused, Class of '47

If I go to the reunion? Of course I'd go to the reunion. You only get an invitation like this once every fifty years or so.

I wondered who'd be at the reunion. How would they look? Would I look as good? What would I wear? Could I lose twenty pounds by June?

Thigh anxiety.

As much as I try to talk myself out of it, my self-esteem seems to decrease as my weight increases.

Once I looked up height and weight charts on the Internet. According to them, I should lose only ten pounds. But when I looked in the mirror, I felt more like Kate Smith than Kate Moss.

Kate Smith   Kate Moss

In elementary school, I was skinny. Then, around my twelfth birthday, that changed, along with a lot of other things.

In junior high, all the popular girls were thin.
In high school, all the thin girls got better dates.
In college, thin girls got engaged first.

When I got married, I wanted to be thin so I'd keep my husband. After a while, I didn't care so much about being thin.

After the divorce, I wanted to be thin so I could get another husband.

Now I wanted to be thin for the reunion. You'd think by now I'd know better—or give up trying.

Some women wear their fat clothes when they can't fit into a size 6. I wear my fat clothes when I can't fit into a size 14.

Does this make me look fat?

Research shows that pretty babies are picked up first.

I daydreamed about being 5'9", weighing 125 pounds, and walking into the reunion.

"Who is *that*?" I imagined Barbara-who-never-wanted-to-play-with-me would say.

Then I'd walk over to Tommy-who-pulled-up-my-skirt-in-second-grade-and-told-everyone-I-wet-my-pants. "Isn't it amazing how some people never change," I'd say. "You're still so short."

Then Ann-the-smart-one would say, "I love your earrings." "They're my Phi Beta Kappa keys," I'd answer.

When it was my turn to say a few words about
what I'd done with my life, I'd skip over 1963,
and everything having to do with my first husband,
certain family relationships, some job disasters,
and my credit card problems.

Everyone would lie. That's what you do at reunions.
People aren't so eager to announce that they had
a face-lift, are on welfare, or regularly attend AA
meetings at the little church around the corner.

I couldn't stop looking at the pictures.

Was there really a time before I was somebody's
wife, somebody's mother, somebody's ex-wife,
somebody's grandmother? A time before now?

I looked at my hand holding the picture—blue veins,
brown spots, wrinkled skin. Once I was eleven
years old.

When I was eleven, I couldn't have imagined being old and worrying about cholesterol. Now I can hardly believe that I was eleven and worried about spelling tests.

When I compare then to now, I liked it better then. But the fact is, the good old days weren't so good when you were going through them.

Dear Olivia,

When I was growing up, life was designed for adults. I was told that children should be seen and not heard. So I was quiet.

It certainly isn't like that today.

I just wanted you to know that you're very lucky to be living now instead of then. I think.

A million hugs and xxxxxxx's,
Grandma

A walk down memory lane could give anyone but Joe Franklin a headache.

Were those happy days when Harry Truman was the president and played "The Missouri Waltz" on the piano, when his daughter Margaret sang, when his wife Bess wore wacky hats?

Harry, Bess, and Margaret.

Dear Bess Truman,

I have always been a fan of yours, even though you look like my Great Aunt Gertrude.

You are the only president's wife who's been alive while I was alive that nobody talks about.

You didn't have cute bangs like Mamie Eisenhower. You weren't a fashion plate like Jackie or Nancy. You never even changed your hairdo.

Didn't anyone ever tell you about makeovers?

Your friend,
Ilene

The next time I was in the city, I found myself driving down the street where my elementary school used to be on 69th Street, off Lexington Avenue. It had been an experimental school for gifted children run by Hunter College.

"Hunter College Elementary School initiated its new policy as a school for the intellectually gifted in 1941 . . . High-I.Q. children residing within specified geographical parameters (including most of Manhattan) were solicited, screened, and selected . . .

Requirements for admission . . . were so stringent that it earned a reputation as one of the most highly selective grade schools in the nation."

— from *Genius Revisited: High IQ Children Grown Up,*
    by Rena Subotnik et al.
    Greenwood Publishing Group, 1993

I think I got in because my older sister got in,
but, to tell you the truth, I think they made a
mistake with her, too.

My sister, of course, would say that I was the
mistake. The day my mother brought me
home from the hospital, she took one look at
me and said, "When is it going back?"

The fact is, I've spent most of my life recovering
from the emotional wounds of my childhood.
Some real. Some not.

Dear Shirley MacLaine,

I have always been a fan of yours throughout your many incarnations.

Could you please tell me if you have—or ever had— sibling rivalry with your brother Warren Beatty?

Your fan,
Ilene

P.S. How come you never had any big romances with other movie stars like everybody else did? Or is there something I don't know about?

My troubles continued in elementary school. The fact is, I lost my self-esteem in kindergarten. At the reunion, I would be face-to-face with the very faces I had envied and feared.

The face I envied most in kindergarten was Patty Parker's. Patty was the prettiest girl in the class.

Everybody wanted to be her best friend. The day Patty picked me to be her best friend was the happiest day of my life. The next day, she picked someone else to be her best friend. I was back to being just me.

Q. *Mirror, mirror on the wall,*
who is the fairest one of all?

A. *Patty Parker.*

Patty always got A's in spelling. Whenever we had a spelling test, I had to go to the bathroom. I'd try to stay there as long as possible. I attributed Patty's ability to win spelling bees to her being pretty.

I remember April 12, 1945, very well. Not because it was the day President Roosevelt died and the country was in mourning, but because it was the day of Patty Parker's tenth birthday party and she had invited me.

I wondered if Patty would be at the reunion.

My elementary-school report cards always said the same thing: "Ilene does not live up to her potential." I figured everybody at the reunion had lived up to their potential. Probably even exceeded it.

Does everyone think that everybody else is doing better?

If only . . .

My mother used to read me stories about girls
who lived up to their potential—Cinderella,
Snow White, Beauty in *Beauty and the Beast*.

Of course some girls, like Cinderella, had to
have a fairy godmother give them a makeover
before they could reach their potential.

Why isn't there even one fairy tale in which
the prince runs off with an overweight girl who
wears glasses?

Betty Grable and her legs.

But even better than fairy tale princesses were
glamour girls. I knew all about them because
every Saturday my Aunt Babbie would take
me to the movies—grown-up movies.

The girls in my class at Hunter were only allowed
to see movies like *Dumbo* and *Bambi.* They didn't
even know that Betty Grable's legs were insured
for a million dollars. They spent Saturdays playing
with dolls.

Why would anyone want to play with a Madame
Alexander doll when you could see Alice Faye in
Technicolor?

Other mothers.

I compared everybody to movie stars. I thought Barbara's mother had a nose like Barbara Stanwyck. Ann's mother was as tall as Ingrid Bergman. Patty's mother put on lipstick like Joan Crawford. Dora's mother had a fur coat like Claudette Colbert. Gay's mother came from Boston and sounded like Katharine Hepburn.

Those mothers never picked up their daughters after school like my mother did. They had important things to do. I wished my mother had important things to do and didn't wait for me after school. My mother didn't get her hair done. She didn't have a fur coat. She didn't even smoke.

I kept hoping that one day I would find out I was
adopted and that my real parents—Ginger Rogers
and Fred Astaire—would come and get me. They'd
buy me fancy evening gowns and we'd all go dancing
in fancy nightclubs—just like in the movies.

Ginger, me, and Fred.

In the movies, just like in fairy tales, beautiful people found other beautiful people and lived happily ever after—Alice Faye found Tyrone Power, Betty Grable found Don Ameche, Rita Hayworth found Victor Mature, Gene Kelly, Glenn Ford, Orson Welles, and a lot of other people.

Zazu Pitts, Margaret Hamilton, and Marjorie Main never found anybody good.

Dear Ava Gardner,

I have always been a fan of yours but you shouldn't have broken up with Frank Sinatra.

Nevertheless, I think you are one of the most beautiful women in the world—at least until you got puffy.

I read that you suffered because you were uneducated and felt stupid. If I had your looks, I wouldn't have cared about being somewhat dumb.

Your fan,
Ilene

My grandfather sold movie magazines in his stationery store. He let me read them for free if I didn't get them dirty.

Reading about Lana Turner's life was a lot more interesting than reading about Pocahontus in school.

In one issue of *Photoplay*, Perc Westmore (who did all the movie stars' makeup) wrote: "The perfect brow is one that conforms to the shape of the eyelid and starts on a line even with the inner corner."

He cautioned, "Beware of angular brows that give a masculine look to the face."

I checked the relationship between the inner corner of my eye and the start of my eyebrow with a ruler. If I frowned, my eyebrows would move down slightly and conform to the shape of my eyelid.

I frowned a lot. I decided it made me look beautiful.

My fourth-grade teacher, Miss Crystal, had
eyebrows that met in the middle.

Miss Crystal never got married. That's what happens
when your eyebrows meet in the middle.

Unless, of course, you're Frida Kahlo.

*Frida Kahlo looked good even though she had a
mustache and didn't tweeze her eyebrows.*

When Miss Crystal was absent, Mrs. Hopkins was our teacher. Mrs. Hopkins wore red lipstick, dangling earrings, jingling bracelets, high heels, and smelled of Evening in Paris perfume. (Miss Crystal smelled like my grandfather.)

If Mrs. Hopkins hadn't been married, somebody would have married her in a minute.

I wondered what memories Olivia would have of her elementary school when she was in her sixties.

When I ask Olivia how's school, she says, "Fine."

She's much more specific when we go shopping.
She'll try on a pair of jeans, make a face in the
mirror, and say, "Gross. They stick out. The
pockets suck. Nobody wears this kind."

"You know," I often will say, "when I was
your age, I thought I looked awful in everything.
But when I look back now . . ."

Before I finish the sentence, Olivia gets that
glazed look in her eyes she always gets whenever
I start a sentence with, "When I was your age."

She must have learned that from her mother.

I read that you're supposed to praise your daughter and tell her she's beautiful even if she looks like Godzilla.

But I also read that a mother's praise can lead to a daughter's having unrealistic expectations.

Whether a mother does or doesn't praise her daughter, her daughter will probably need years of therapy.

"*It is most unfortunate that my sons have such long eyelashes while my daughter hasn't any at all.*"

—Queen Elizabeth II

Dear Jacqueline Kennedy Onassis,

I have always been a fan of yours.

I read that your mother always told you that your hairline was too low, that your eyes were too far apart, and that you weren't feminine enough.

I just wanted you to know that she was wrong.

Your fan,
Ilene

I was on my daughter's case a lot, too.
"Why don't you wear lipstick?"
"I think you'd look better with shorter hair."
"Maybe you should tweeze your eyebrows
in the middle more."

Whenever she saw me with a red lipstick in my
hand, she'd run, fearful that next would come the
blue eye shadow, the kohl eyeliner, and the
eyelash curler, and I'd re-create Max Factor circa
1953 on her face.

No wonder my daughter didn't have more
self-esteem.

Max Factor, circa 1953.

Dear Olivia,

You probably won't understand much about
this letter, but since I'm never going to send it to you,
that's all right.

I just got off the phone with your mother. I can
tell from her voice that she's mad at me.

It always amazes me how little influence I
have on making her happy, and how much influence
I have on making her unhappy.

I was watching a television program this morning
and a famous psychologist was telling everybody that
happiness is a state of mind. I haven't a clue as to how
to drive to that state.

But whenever I'm sad, I think about you—and
then I smile. Maybe that psychologist knew something
after all.

A million hugs and xxxxxxx's,
Grandma

When you have daughters, you start to worry about their looks.

I found myself passing on to my daughters things my mother had told me:

> *Never order meatloaf in a restaurant.*
> *You never know what they put in it.*
>
> *Never order a papaya drink. They never*
> *clean the tanks.*
>
> *Never walk on a subway grating. You*
> *might fall in.*
>
> *If you look beautiful, you'll live happily*
> *ever after.*

Dear Sarah Jessica Parker,
Gwyneth Paltrow, and
Kate Hudson,

I have always been a fan of yours. Now that you are mothers, I have two pieces of advice for you because I'm a mother too.

Number 1: Husbands come and go but children are forever.

Number 2: Don't worry that when your babies grow up they're not as skinny as you are. They can still be happy.

Your fan,
Ilene

In my youthful pursuit of glamour, I had my
ears pierced in junior high school. I thought
it would make me look exotic. Like Yvonne de Carlo.
A doctor pierced them. I got an infection anyway.

I had to do something daring. I was the only girl in
eighth-grade gym class who still wore an undershirt.
Even though I'd spent hours trying to make my
elbows touch in back so my front would grow,
nothing moved.

When I look at my chest now, I realize I didn't need
to exercise so much.

The summer I was thirteen, Eileen Ford, the head of the Ford Model Agency, had a radio program on Saturdays at one o'clock on which she'd reveal the beauty secrets of famous models.

Listeners could write her letters about their beauty problems, and she'd pick some to answer on the air. She wouldn't use the person's name if she read their letter. I wrote her a letter.

One Saturday, I was eating a can of Franco-American spaghetti and listening to her program when she read a letter about someone with all my beauty problems: bitten nails, shiny nose, stringy hair, flat-chested, big feet, bony knees, buck teeth, near-sighted, and shy.

I got so nervous, I ran out of the kitchen. A minute later, I went back to listen. By then, she was reading somebody else's problems.

I always wondered if my life would have turned out differently if I'd heard her advice.

Even Anne Frank complained about her looks. In 1942 she wrote in her diary:*

The 7 or 12 beautiful features (not mine mind you!) should come here, then I can fill in which ones I have, and which ones I don't.

1. *blue eyes, black hair (no.)*
2. *dimples in cheeks (yes.)*
3. *dimple in chin (yes.)*
4. *widow's peak (no.)*
5. *white skin (yes.)*
6. *straight teeth (no.)*
7. *small mouth (no.)*
8. *curly eyelashes (no.)*
9. *straight nose (yes.) {at least so far.}*
10. *nice clothes (sometimes.) {not nearly enough in my opinion.}*
11. *nice fingernails (sometimes.)*
12. *intelligent (sometimes.)*

*from *The Diary of Anne Frank: The Critical Edition.*
Edited by David Barnouw and Gerrold Van Der Stroom. Doubleday, 1989

Dear Olivia,

    I just got home from ShopRite. While I was waiting on the checkout line, I picked up a magazine that had one of those really famous models on the cover. I know her face but not her name.

    No real women look like that.

    I just wanted you to know that in case you thought they did.

                    A million hugs and xxxxxxx's,
                    Grandma

Who made up all the rules on how girls are supposed to look? Why do we believe them?

Today Botticelli's Venus would wear a size 16.

Even though my high school was all girls,
we were always checking each other out.

Every day it was the same thing:
Who had the best hair.
Who wore the best outfit.
Who got the best grade.
If I got a good grade but my hair wasn't good
that day, I felt like a failure.

It was always easy to find something wrong
with myself starting with my overbite and
working my way down to my size 9½ shoes.

Dear Gene Tierney,

> *I have always been a fan of yours.*
> Laura *was once my favorite movie.*
> *We have something in common—an overbite.*
> *You looked so beautiful in* Leave Her to
> Heaven, *especially in that violet dress, no wonder*
> *Cornel Wilde was clueless that you were a murderer.*

> *Your friend,*
> *Ilene*

Everywhere I'd go, in every movie, on every magazine page, I'd see a beautiful girl staring at me and I'd compare myself to her—Miss Rheingold, the Breck Shampoo girl, Miss Subways. (I heard they're bringing Miss Subways back— just what we need!)

At least they were dressed. Poor Olivia. She's got Britney Spears to contend with.

Dear Olivia,

    I was trying to find something to watch on television and I looked at the MTV channel by mistake. I couldn't believe my eyes.

    Kids seemed to be doing things to music that I didn't know about until after I was married . . . and I certainly never did to music.

    I just wanted you to know that.

                A million hugs and xxxxxx's,
                Grandma

Dear Madonna,

I have always been a fan of yours even though at first I liked Cyndi Lauper better.

I wondered if you could tell me which of your looks you liked best. Also, what would you do if your daughter Lourdes dyed her hair a lot and dressed like you?

Your fan,
Ilene

Madonna

Top Twelve People Admired by Teenagers, 1950 *Life* Magazine Survey	Olivia's Top Twelve List, 2004
1. Louisa May Alcott	1. Olivia Newton-John
2. Joe DiMaggio	2. My mom
3. Vera-Ellen	3. My sister Allie
4. Franklin D. Roosevelt	4. My sister Emma
5. Abraham Lincoln	5. Jason Kidd
6. Roy Rogers	6. Mrs. Sperduto (fifth-grade teacher)
7. Douglas MacArthur	7. Jessica Simpson
8. Clara Barton	8. Vin Diesel
9. Doris Day	9. William Hung (American Idol nonwinner)
10. Sister Kenny	10. Eddie Murphy
11. Babe Ruth	11. Nick Lachey (Jessica Simpson's husband)
12. Florence Nightingale	12. John Travolta

I remember I once wrote a note to myself: "Do not overvalue others and undervalue yourself." But I didn't take my own advice.

Instead, I looked to *Cosmopolitan* magazine for advice.

> *Dear Helen Gurley Brown,*
>
> *I've always been a fan of yours. You were way ahead of the times when you told women not to be mousey back in the 1970s. I was a mouse.*
>
> *I am sorry to tell you, however, that* Cosmopolitan *magazine has done more harm to my self-esteem than Yodels and Mallomars have done to my waistline.*
>
> *I tried all your tips and followed all your instructions, but I always ended up still being me.*
>
> *Nevertheless, I appreciate your efforts.*
>
> *Your friend,*
> *Ilene*

*"Nearly every glamorous, wealthy, successful career woman
you envy now started out as some kind of schlep."*

—Helen Gurley Brown,
Founding Editor, *Cosmopolitan* magazine

My high-school English teacher, Miss Burstein, once read a passage from *The Bell Jar.*

I identified with everything Sylvia Plath's character Esther Greenwood said:

> *I started adding up all the things I couldn't do . . .*
> *I began with cooking . . .*
> *I didn't know shorthand either . . .*
> *I was a terrible dancer . . .*
> *I couldn't carry a tune . . .*
> *I had no sense of balance . . .*
> *I couldn't ride a horse or ski . . .*
> *I couldn't speak German or read Hebrew*
> *or write Chinese . . .*

But my list would have been a lot longer.

One morning, I got a surprise email from Mimi Goodman. She had been my best friend in elementary school. She'd gotten my email address from someone on the reunion committee.

Dear Ilene,

Do you remember me from Hunter? I had dirty blond hair that wouldn't curl. Are you still skinny? I live in California. Are you going to the reunion? I hope you are and that you'll email me back.

Mimi Goodman

I emailed her right back.

Dear Mimi,

I'm so happy to hear from you. Of course I remember you and your hair. You don't have to worry. I'm not skinny anymore.

Please email me back everything that's happened to you in the past fifty years. I'll go to the reunion if my diet works.

Ilene

How could I not remember Mimi? We had played doctor all through kindergarten. Mimi had more trading cards than I had, and she was better at hopscotch. Nevertheless, I liked her.

In fifth grade, when we played in Central Park, we always checked out the illuminated sign at the Essex House on Central Park South. Once the first two letters didn't light up and Mimi and I laughed our heads off.

Mimi and I started emailing regularly. In one email, she confessed that she'd been in awe of Patty Parker.

I had thought I was the only one.

One time Mimi and I went to see the movie *Good News.* June Allyson played the ingenue (she always played the ingenue—until recently when she did commercials for incontinence products).

The night of the movie I went to sleep with curlers in my hair and came to school the next day with my hair in a pageboy like June. Mimi was mean to me that day.

Most of the time I'd go to Mimi's house after school and we'd read *Seventeen* magazines.

In one email, Mimi wrote about how well she remembered my mother.

I had been so ashamed of my mother for all the things she wasn't.

"You were lucky," Mimi wrote. "She was always there for you, always waiting for you after school, to take you to Central Park."

I wish I could have told my mother what Mimi said—and a lot of other things.

I was so happy to have Mimi as a friend again.
Girlfriends make life a lot easier to get through.
Especially as you get older and you know you
can turn to them for understanding when husbands,
children, job problems, or general bad luck
screw up your life.

Especially when you know that their lives haven't
been perfect either.

Dear Olivia,

I just ran into my friend while I was taking my winter coat to the cleaners. You don't know her.

I haven't seen her in a while and she told me about her recent surgery.

I used to think that beauty brought happiness but I was wrong. Good health brings happiness.

I just wanted you to know that.

A million hugs and xxxxxxx's,
Grandma

The reunion was now only two months away. I couldn't stop thinking about it. It was like a movie that I watched over and over again in my head. Sophia Loren played me. I kept changing my mind about what we'd wear.

"But I'm not beautiful, certainly not in a glamorous sense. My nose is too big and pointed. My mouth is too large. My profile is without distinction."

—Sophia Loren

Dear Sophia Loren,

I've always been a fan of yours.

You probably don't know it, but we have something in common—we're the same age, except you look better.

I have two questions:

1) If you didn't have your own line of eyeglasses, would you still wear glasses? I wear contacts.

2) Do you look like Sophia Loren when you wake up in the morning, before you pencil in your eyebrows?

I know you are probably busy getting yourself so beautiful, so I'm enclosing a self-addressed stamped envelope for your answers.

Your friend,
Ilene

It's hard to give up wanting to look good even when you're a senior citizen. The problem is, the older you get, the more work it takes.

Sometimes I wish I were a man. What they look like, once they're out of high school, doesn't seem to matter.

For a woman, there's always something to fix. I don't think it's just me. Ask any woman what she would change about herself and she'll probably come up with a list.

Ask any man what he'd like to change and he'll probably say his job.

Men don't have to look good.

Men aren't as hard on themselves or on other men as women are on themselves and on other women.

When a man walks down the street, he doesn't critique other men's hairdos.

Women compare everything about each other and judge each other by impossible standards. We think we have to be perfect at everything. It's like being back in high school and having to get good grades, and have a cute boyfriend, and have good hair.

What's funny for me to look at these pictures now is to think how much I wasn't nearly as ugly as I thought I was, and so much of feeling insecure is meaningless... Because there I was, perfectly lovely.

Anjelica Huston

I've always checked out other women. I do it on movie lines, at ShopRite, in McDonald's. I think to myself:

- That's the wrong hairstyle for her.
- Doesn't that woman have a full-length mirror at home?
- Oh, blondie, you need your roots done.
- Those shoes have seen too many rainy days.
- Dangling rhinestone earrings don't go with sneakers.
- Nobody will take you seriously with those nails.
- Hey, missy, it's time to call Jenny Craig.
- No one looks good in that color.

It's all I can do to stop myself from walking over to a total stranger and saying, "Honey, lose the horizontal stripes."

"*You see someone on the street and essentially what you notice about them is the flaw.*"

—Diane Arbus

Dear Goldie Hawn,

I've always been a fan of yours but I have to tell you something—stop trying to look like your daughter's sister.

Enough plastic surgery! Cut your hair. Look how much better Jane Fonda looks without the Barbarella do. Give up the spaghetti-strap dresses. Even with a personal trainer, you can't exercise away flapping upper arms.

Only a mother who cares about you could tell you the truth, and I'm a mother.

Your friend,
Ilene

P.S. Also, stop shaking your booty. Over fifty, nobody's booty is cute.

I only wished I could have walked into the
reunion looking half as good as Goldie Hawn.

I used to look in the mirror a lot more than I
do now. Now I don't recognize the person I see
looking back at me.

The worst mirrors are in ladies' rooms where
the lights are always too bright. Some things it's
better not to see.

I still watch the Miss America contest, mostly to criticize.

Elizabeth Taylor would never have won. Her legs are too short.

I wonder if she would have stayed married to Richard Burton if she'd had longer legs.

Dear Elizabeth Taylor,

I have always been a fan of yours, and no matter how much you weigh, I think you're beautiful.

I have always admired your courage but not always your taste in men. I'm glad that you and Debbie finally became friends. It's hard to believe that you both were once married to Eddie Fisher.

Your friend,
Ilene

P.S. Do you tweeze or wax your eyebrows?

I realized long ago that reading magazines
to find answers to beauty problems was
useless. The advice they give in the twenty-first
century is no different from the advice
they gave in the 1950s: don't use soap on
your face, drink lots of water, and
moisturize.

It cost fifteen cents to learn that from a
magazine in 1957, sixty cents in 1971, and
almost four dollars in 2004.

My husband never reads magazines to find out how to improve himself. He's never coveted Sean Connery's beauty secrets.

My husband's had the same hairdo for twenty-five years, even though now he has a lot less hair.

When he looks in the mirror, he's not looking for imperfections—he's just glad to see that his reflection is still there.

Why is it men love women's bodies so much and women hate their bodies so much?

Whenever I ask my husband if I look fat, he says no. In comparison to him, I'm not. But I see who he looks at when we walk down the street.

He's even said I look good without makeup. Of course, he only sees me without makeup twice a day. When I wake up in the morning and just before I go to sleep at night. Both times he's not wearing his glasses.

"But a girl's best beauty aid is still a near-sighted man."

—Yoko Ono

Once I dreamed I was in a fancy mall. It was probably the Short Hills Mall in New Jersey. The stores were all boutiques selling designer body parts.

I charged a pair of Manolo Blahnik feet, a Chanel chin, and a perfectly matched set of boobs designed by Vera Wang exclusively for me. On my way out, I picked up a Versace midriff on sale. For the first time in my life, I was finally perfect.

When I got home, my husband took one look at the bill and returned me.

My husband doesn't judge all women by how they compare to Audrey Hepburn. His standards are simpler. He requests only four things:

1. I don't look too weird.
2. I don't nag.
3. I cook sometimes.
4. We have sex a lot.

If I did all these things, he'd think I was the most beautiful woman in the world.

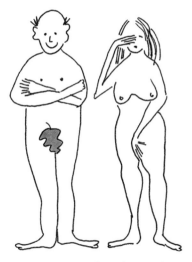

Studies show men are anxious about their performance during sex.
Women are anxious about how they look.

Dear Audrey Hepburn,

I have always been a fan of yours. I have seen **Breakfast at Tiffany's** *many times even though I don't like cats.*

When I was in high school, I had eyebrows like you. I could show you a picture. I think I plucked them too much because now they're as thin as Greta Garbo's (but I don't look like her).

I always wanted to look like you. Everybody wants to look like you. What's it like to be perfect?

Your friend,
Ilene

"She was terribly insecure about her bustline, but I told her people would look at her eyes first, no matter what size her breasts were."

—Givenchy, about Audrey Hepburn

My husband doesn't understand why you'd want to look like Audrey Hepburn if you could look like Marilyn Monroe.

There are so many things he doesn't understand. For instance, he doesn't understand why, if I have one red lipstick, I would buy another. Or why I would need another pair of black shoes. He doesn't understand why anyone would choose to have surgery just to have a body part made bigger or smaller.

Freud didn't understand women either. Nobody understands women except other women.

Dear Marilyn Monroe,

I've always been a fan of yours.

I read that you were friendly and loving and not stuck-up. So even if you looked like the Elephant Man and were always late for everything, I would have been your friend.

If you got sad or lonely, you could have called me up. I would have come right over with some Rocky Road ice cream. We could have played gin rummy and sung camp songs and made phony phone calls. I would have polished your nails every color, even your toenails. I'd sleep over and then, in the morning, we could have gone out for pancakes and then bought shoes.

Your friend,
Ilene

P.S. Did you ever want to look like Audrey Hepburn?

Two weeks before the reunion, Mimi emailed—

Urgent . . . do you think the reunion can
be postponed? I got my hair cut this morning
by a sadistic beautician and I can't leave
the house until it grows back.

I understood perfectly. I'd lived through WWII, witnessed man walking on the moon, the assassinations of JFK, RFK, and Martin Luther King, Jr. Watergate, impeachment, and terrorist attacks. And I still don't know what to do with my hair.

"I remember Hillary telling me at a luncheon that she was amazed at the interest in her hairdos. 'I'm stuck with a certain figure. If I could change anything, it would be my legs, but I can't, so I change my hair.'"

—Anna Wintour, in *Vogue*

"I have very blonde eyelashes and very dark hair . . . I bleach everything that's dark and I dye everything that's blonde."

—Angie Dickinson

"Never blow dry hair, that's really bad for it. I just towel dry it, and I only wash it once a week, because I like the oil. And if you leave your hair dirty after a while it stops becoming dirtier."

—Jerry Hall

Doris Day had great hair. It's no wonder she was always smiling.

Who hasn't had hair problems? People with straight hair always want curls and vice versa. People with short hair always want long hair. And vice versa.

I once got my hair cut like Mia Farrow in *Rosemary's Baby.* What was I thinking?

Mia Farrow

Whistler's Mother

Carmen Miranda

Mother Teresa

Amelia Earhart

Indira Gandhi

Queen Victoria

Bad hair days throughout history.

Dear Meryl Streep,

I have always been a fan of yours.

I think you are the most versatile actress because of all the accents you can do and all the wigs you wear.

I once wore a wig to a costume party and it gave me a really bad headache.

I think you are aging very well unlike some other movie stars who had dreadful face-lifts (you know who I mean).

Your fan,
Ilene

P.S. I think it's stupid to call actresses actors. Please remind everybody that they give the Oscar to the Best Actor and the Best Actress not to the Best Actor and the Best Actor. Thank you.

*I've never seen a picture of Eve where she didn't
look like she had hair extensions.*

I've made a lot of beauty mistakes besides my Mia Farrow haircut. My makeup junk drawer is filled with impulse items I've bought. The colors looked gorgeous on the models in the ads.

The drawer is also full of coral-colored lipsticks, blushes, and foundations that were included in gift packages from cosmetics companies. I've kept them, even though forty years ago, a saleswoman at the Helena Rubinstein counter at Bloomingdale's told me, "Never wear makeup with an orange base. You have sallow skin." I keep hoping that one day I'll wake up and I won't have sallow skin.

In all probability, I'll still have sallow skin when I'm a hundred. In all probability, it will even be sallower. But I'll probably still have that drawerful.

No one really cares how you look when you get older anyway, as long as you close your mouth when you chew and don't drool.

But every few years somebody does research and once again discovers that beautiful people have an advantage in life, taller people get better jobs, thinner people are more successful.

Even though I know better, I still fuss with eyeliners, blow dryers, and diets, hoping I'll become better looking, taller, thinner, and happier.

Who lives without contradictions?
But who wants to live without hope?

Sunday nights are usually my beauty nights—
even though Monday mornings I don't look
any different.

When I looked in the mirror the morning of
the reunion, there was so much work I had to
do to my face to get ready to face the day.

Natural beauties must have so much extra
time in the morning.

"You dont' have to be dowdy to be a Christian."

—Tammy Faye Bakker

As I drove into the city the day of the reunion,
I kept looking in the visor mirror.

Was there lipstick on my teeth?
Maybe I should have worn the blue dress
instead.

Maybe I should have stayed home.

What should I make
for dinner?

How will I compare
to my classmates?

Pray for peace.

Who should win
the Oscars?

Are the children
okay?

Pie chart inside my head.

I got to the reunion early. As I walked in, someone handed me a nametag. It was printed in large type.

The room was filled with people I didn't recognize. I thought they looked a lot older than me.

A woman across the room was staring at me. She started walking over and, when she got closer, I noticed her straight-as-sticks, gray hair. Then I saw her nametag.

That couldn't be Mimi, the girl I had played hopscotch with in Central Park. What had happened to her? She looked like somebody's grandmother.

Was she thinking the same thing about me? After all, I am somebody's grandmother.

Once we had been beautiful children jumping rope, playing hide-and-seek, going to birthday parties.

Now we were both old women, our pasts much longer than our futures.

All those years had gone by so quickly. Why hadn't somebody stopped the clocks? But when?
In elementary school? In high school? Yesterday?
Right now? When was it best?

My head filled with a lifetime of memories.

Suddenly, Mimi and I were hugging and laughing. Other people were, too. The "boys" not as much.

Joanie Bettis, who had been the best dodge ball player in the class, walked up to me and told me she wanted to apologize. I had no idea what for. She said that when we were in sixth grade, she had taunted me with a ham sandwich, knowing that my grandparents, whom I lived with, were kosher. She said she'd felt guilty about it ever since 1947.

I forgave her—even though I don't remember it ever happening.

Patty Parker didn't show up. Somebody
who'd been in touch with her said she'd been
having marital and financial problems.

Ann, the smart one, revealed how insecure
she'd felt all through school.

I even found out I wasn't the only one whose
family had been poor.

Throughout the evening, my classmates spoke
about things we'd never read about in fairy tales—
mothers who drank, fathers who were unfaithful.
Mary Ellen's brother killed himself.

I thought I had known so much about them.

I had expected everyone at the reunion to have lived an extraordinary life. Some did. Our class included doctors, lawyers, big-deal bankers, financial wizards, a judge, several Ph.D's, and a mother of six.

But our class also included someone with a handicapped child, someone who'd had a double mastectomy, someone who'd had a triple bypass, someone who'd wanted children but couldn't conceive, someone whose child had died.

Careers had been unfulfilled. Marriages had ended. One of my classmates had been institutionalized.

Standing there, in the middle of the room, with chicken salad, salmon mousse, and poached pears on my plate, and holding a glass of Perrier with a twist of lime, it didn't matter who looked prettier, or who was thinner, or what anyone was wearing. I didn't want to change places with anyone.

There wasn't anyone who hadn't had losses and regrets in their life—including me. But we were the lucky ones—three of our classmates were dead.

Once we all had been considered the luckiest
children in the city. We had been told we were
the brightest, the most gifted. We were full of hopes
and dreams. Fifty years of life had changed us all.

My class in 2001.

After four hours of reminiscing, most of us had nothing left to say to one another.

I exchanged telephone numbers and email addresses with a few people. We said we'd be in touch, but I knew we wouldn't.

Saying goodbye wasn't easy. I think we all knew there would never be another reunion of the Hunter Elementary School class of 1947.

Driving home, I thought about my own life. A line from a Billy Joel song popped into my head, and I started humming, "I like you just the way you are."

I wondered if Billy Joel sang that song to the supermodel he was married to. I wondered why they got divorced.

Life never turns out the way anyone expects.

Dear Olivia,

There are a lot of things I wish I'd known when I was your age.

I wish I'd known that not everyone had a wonderful childhood.

I wish I'd known that people liked me just the way I was, even if I didn't like me the way I was.

I wish I'd known that I already had everything I needed within myself to be happy, instead of looking for happiness at the beauty counters of Bloomingdale's.

It takes a lifetime to get smart—even for a Hunter Elementary School graduate.

I just wanted you to know that.

A million hugs and xxxxxxx's,
Grandma

"What a wonderful life I've had.
I only wish I'd realized it sooner."

—Colette

In memory of my friend Dorothy Lohman
1915–2002